# ESSENTIAL ELEMENTS

**LEVEL FOUR**

# PIANO THEORY

ISBN 978-1-4768-0611-2

**HAL•LEONARD®**
CORPORATION

7777 W. BLUEMOUND RD. P.O. BOX 13819 MILWAUKEE, WI 53213

In Australia Contact:
**Hal Leonard Australia Pty. Ltd.**
4 Lentara Court
Cheltenham, Victoria, 3192 Australia
Email: ausadmin@halleonard.com.au

Visit Hal Leonard Online at
**www.halleonard.com**

# To the Student

I wrote these books with you in mind. As a young student I often wondered how completing theory workbooks would make me a better musician. The theory work often seemed separate from the music I was playing. My goal in *Essential Elements Piano Theory* is to provide you with the tools you will need to compose, improvise, play classical and popular music, or to better understand any other musical pursuit you might enjoy. In each "Musical Mastery" section of this book you will experience creative applications of the theory you have learned. The "Ear Training" pages will be completed with your teacher at the lesson. In this series you will begin to learn the building blocks of music, which make it possible for you to have fun at the piano. A practical understanding of theory enables you to see what is possible in music. I wish you all the best on your journey as you learn the language of music!

Sincerely,
Mona Rejino

# To the Teacher

I believe that knowledge of theory is most beneficial when a concept is followed directly by a musical application. In *Essential Elements Piano Theory*, learning theory becomes far more than completing worksheets. Students have the opportunity to see why learning a particular concept can help them become a better pianist right away. They can also see how the knowledge of musical patterns and chord progressions will enable them to be creative in their own musical pursuits: composing, arranging, improvising, playing classical and popular music, accompanying, or any other.

A free download of the *Teacher's Answer Key* is available at www.halleonard.com/eeptheory4answer.

# Acknowledgements

I would like to thank Hal Leonard Corporation for providing me the opportunity to put these theoretical thoughts down on paper and share them with others. I owe a debt of gratitude to Jennifer Linn, who has helped with this project every step of the way. These books would not have been possible without the support of my family: To my husband, Richard, for his wisdom and amazing ability to solve dilemmas; to my children, Maggie and Adam, for helping me think outside the box.

# TABLE OF CONTENTS

## REVIEW

1. Write the number of beats each note or rest receives in $\frac{4}{4}$ time.

2. Draw these notes or rests in the boxes.

quarter note =                              whole note =

dotted half note =                         half note =

whole rest =                               eighth rest =

eighth note =                              half rest =

quarter rest =                             two eighth notes =

3. Write the counts under each measure in the examples below. *The first measure is done for you.* Clap and count each rhythm aloud.

4. In the blanks below the staff, name the distance between each pair of notes. Use **W** for whole step, **H** for half step, and **0** for no step (enharmonic).

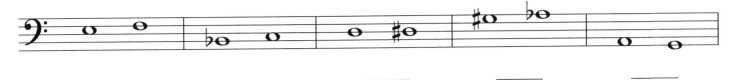

_____  _____  _____  _____  _____

_____  _____  _____  _____  _____

5. Circle the two notes that form a half step in each example.

6. Circle the two notes that form a whole step in each example.

7. Two Major 5-finger patterns and triads are given below. In the blank staff, write the corresponding minor 5-finger pattern and triad. _Lower the third note one half step._

### D Major 5-Finger Pattern   Triad

### D minor 5-Finger Pattern   Triad

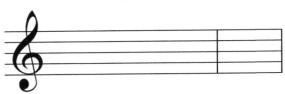

### F Major 5-Finger Pattern   Triad

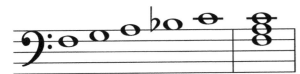

### F minor 5-Finger Pattern   Triad

5

8. Complete the Major and minor 5-finger patterns on each staff. Mark the half steps with a curved line. *The half step is between notes 3 and 4 in a Major 5-finger pattern. The half step is between notes 2 and 3 in a minor 5-finger pattern.*

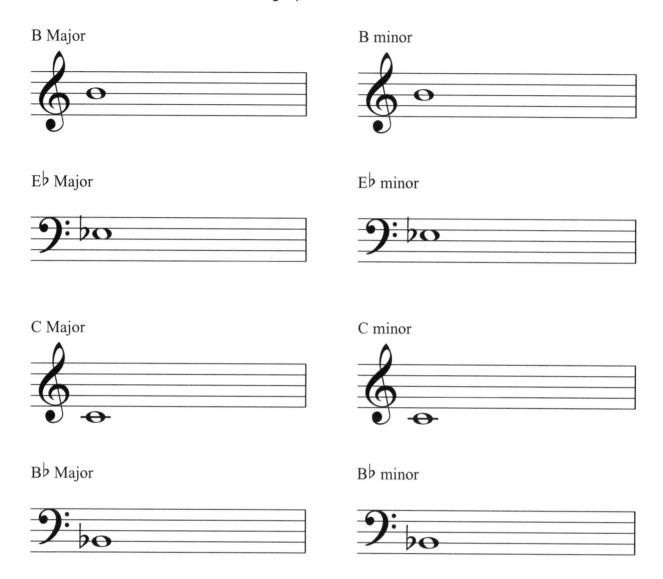

9. Six Major triads are given below. Fill in the second measure with the minor triad. *Lower the 3rd one half step.*

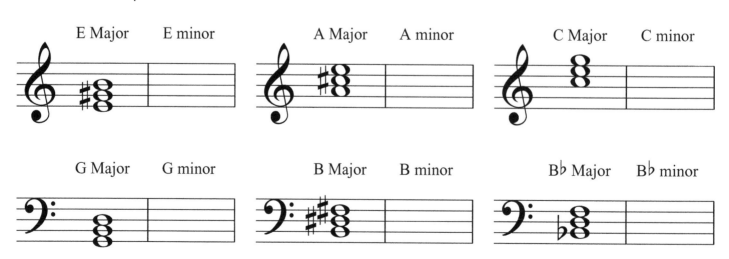

# Rhythm and Upbeats

♩. A **DOTTED QUARTER NOTE** = 1-1/2 beats of sound

A dot after a note adds half the value of the note.

1  +  ½

The dotted quarter note is usually followed by a single eighth note.

♩.  ♪  =  2 beats

A dotted quarter note is equal to a quarter note tied to an eighth note.

The tied eighth note is replaced by the dot.

Count: 1  +  2  +    1  +  2  +

1. Rewrite these rhythms by replacing ♩⌣♩♩ with ♩. ♪. *The first one is done for you.*

Write the counts under each rhythm, then clap and count each rhythm aloud.

2. Write the correct time signature in the boxes for each rhythm below. Choose from $\frac{2}{4}$, $\frac{3}{4}$ and $\frac{4}{4}$.

3. Add the missing bar lines to the rhythms. Write the counts below each measure. Choose one key on the piano and play each example while counting aloud.

4. Draw a line connecting the boxes that have the same number of beats.

An **UPBEAT** is one or more notes that come before the first full measure of a piece.

When a piece begins with an upbeat (pick-up notes), the missing beats are found in the last measure. Add the upbeat to the beats in the incomplete last measure to make one full measure.

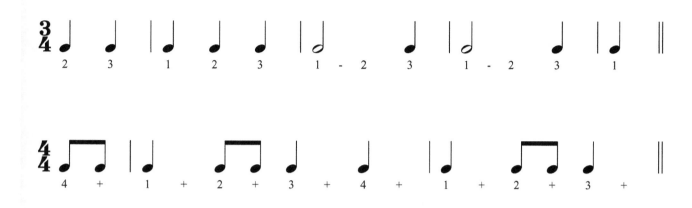

5. Write the correct time signature in each box. Write the counts under each measure. Play each melody, repeating it once.

# Ledger Line Note Reading

**LEDGER LINES** are short lines added above or below the staff. Ledger lines continue the pattern of lines and spaces to extend the range of the staff.

Notice that Bass Clef C's and Treble Clef C's are a mirror image of each other.

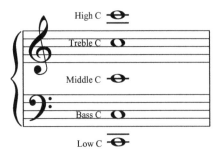

1. Locate and play Low C, Bass C, Middle C, Treble C and High C on the keyboard. *Each C is one octave (eight keys) from the other.*

2. Find and play the following Ledger Line and Space Notes.

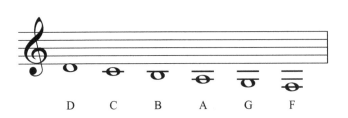

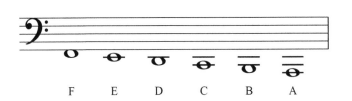

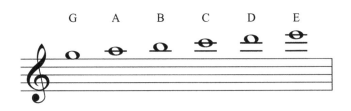

3. Trace three C's in different octaves.

Draw three B's in different octaves.

Draw three A's in different octaves.

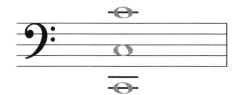
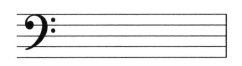
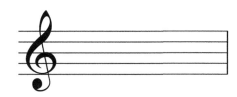

Draw three D's in different octaves.

Draw three F's in different octaves.

Draw three G's in different octaves.

Draw three E's in different octaves.

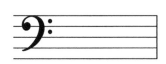

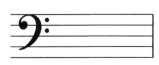

4. In each example, fill in the blanks to spell a word.

_____ _____ _____

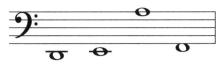
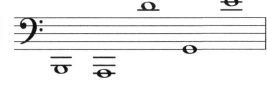

_____ _____ _____ _____

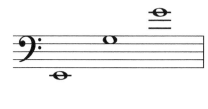
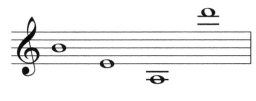
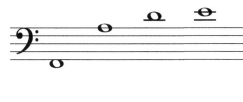

_____ _____ _____

# MUSICAL MASTERY

## Ear Training

1. You will hear four measures of rhythmic dictation. Fill in the blank measures with the rhythm you hear.

2. You will hear one rhythm from each pair. Circle the rhythm you hear.

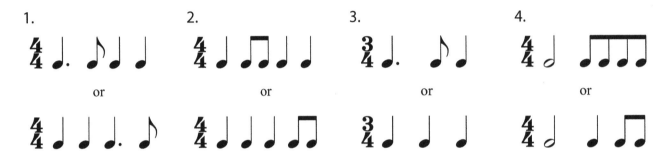

3. You will hear four measures of melodic dictation using notes from the C Major 5-finger pattern. Fill in the blank measures with the rhythms and pitches you hear.

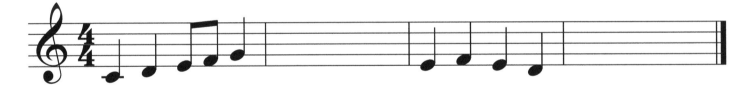

4. The first example in each pair is Major. The second example in each pair is minor. Circle the one you hear.

# Reading Mastery

1. Play the three musical excerpts below, then answer the questions.

### 1. G Major Pattern

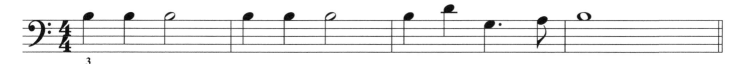

### 2. E Minor Pattern

### 3. F Major Pattern

    a.  Which melody begins with an upbeat? _____

    b.  Which melodies have an interval of a 5th? _____

    c.  Which melodies have an interval of a 3rd? _____

    d.  Which melodies use the dotted quarter/eighth note rhythm? _____

    e.  Which melodies use ledger lines? _____

    f.  Can you name any of the musical excerpts? (*Answers at the bottom of page)

    _____

2. Transpose each melody above to another pattern. Choose from these 5-finger patterns:

       C Major         D Major         A Major         F minor         G minor

The use of ledger lines allows you to explore the full range of the keyboard. In "Cave Explorers" measures 1–6 use notes in the C Major triad. Measures 9–14 use notes in the A minor triad.

1. Play "Cave Explorers."

# Cave Explorers

Mona Rejino

# Intervals

An **INTERVAL** is the distance between two keys or notes.

**MELODIC INTERVALS** are two notes played separately to make a melody.

2nd    3rd    4th    5th

**HARMONIC INTERVALS** are two notes played together to make a harmony.

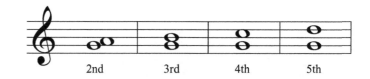

2nd    3rd    4th    5th

1. In the box below each pair of notes, name the interval. In the blank, label the interval either melodic or harmonic.

On the keyboard, an interval of a 6th skips four keys.

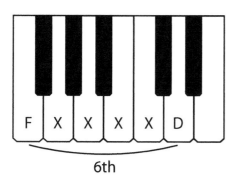

6th

On the staff, an interval of a 6th skips four notes.

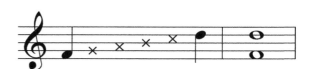

2. Draw a melodic 6th up or down from the given note. Name each note.

up a 6th    down a 6th    down a 6th    up a 6th    down a 6th

3. Draw a harmonic 6th up or down from the given note.

up a 6th      down a 6th      up a 6th      up a 6th      down a 6th

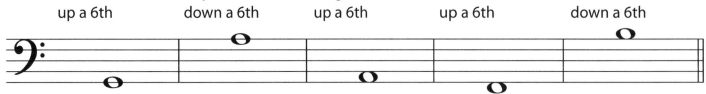

On the keyboard, an interval of a 7th skips five keys.

On the staff, an interval of a 7th skips five notes.

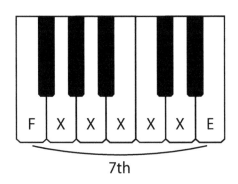

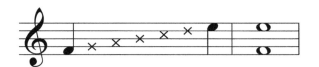

4. Draw a melodic 7th up or down from the given note. Name each note.

up a 7th      down a 7th      up a 7th      down a 7th      up a 7th

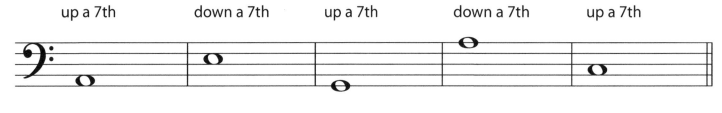

_____ _____ _____ _____ _____ _____ _____ _____ _____ _____

5. Draw a harmonic 7th up or down from the given note.

down a 7th      up a 7th      up a 7th      down a 7th      down a 7th

On the keyboard, an interval of an octave (8th) skips six keys.

On the staff, an interval of an octave (8th) skips six notes.

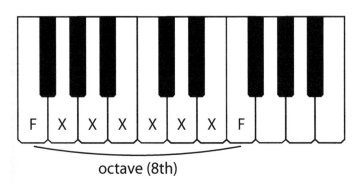

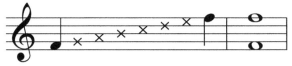

6. Draw a melodic octave (8th) up or down from the given note. Name each note.

up an 8th      down an 8th      up an 8th      down an 8th      up an 8th

___   ___   ___   ___   ___   ___   ___   ___   ___   ___

7. Draw a harmonic octave (8th) up or down from the given note.

down an 8th      up an 8th      up an 8th      down an 8th      up an 8th

Intervals that move from **line to space** or **space to line** are always even numbers: 2nds, 4ths, 6ths or 8ths

Intervals that move from **line to line** or **space to space** are always odd numbers: 3rds, 5ths or 7ths

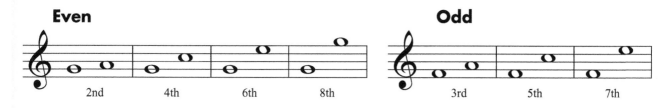

8. In the box below each note, write L for line note and S for space note. In the blank, name the interval.

___   ___   ___   ___   ___   ___   ___   ___   ___   ___

9. Name each interval (6th, 7th or 8th).

___   ___   ___   ___   ___   ___   ___   ___

# UNIT 5

## Major Scales

A **MAJOR SCALE** is made up of eight consecutive notes (scale degrees) arranged in the following pattern of whole steps and half steps:

The half steps are between scale degrees 3-4 and 7-8.

The first note of a scale is called the **keynote** or **tonic**.

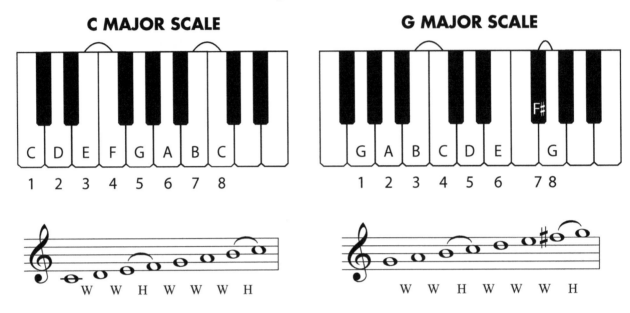

1.  Complete the C Major scale. Mark the half steps with a curved line.

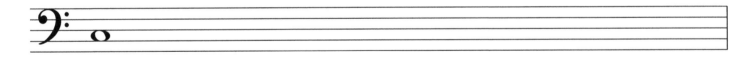

2.  Complete the G Major scale. Mark the half steps with a curved line.

3. Add the correct sharps to form a D Major scale. *Use the Major scale pattern: W W H W W W H*
   Mark the half steps with a curved line.

4. Add the correct flat to form an F Major scale. Mark the half steps with a curved line.

5. Add the correct flat to form a B♭ Major scale. Mark the half steps with a curved line.

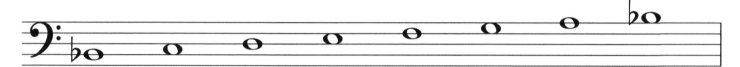

6. Complete the C Major scale in the two octaves given on the grand staff. *The first and last notes of each scale are written for you.*

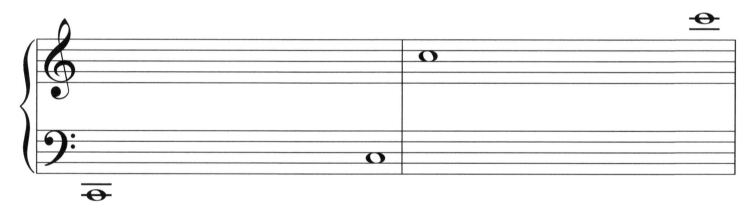

7. Complete each Major scale in the two octaves given on the grand staff. Add accidentals where needed.

**G Major Scale**

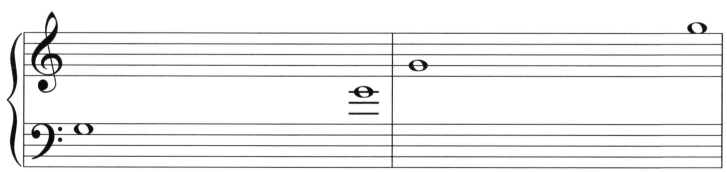

**D Major Scale**

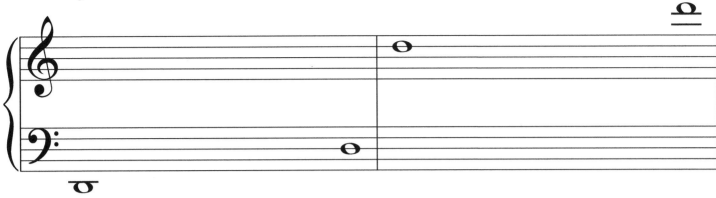

**F Major Scale**

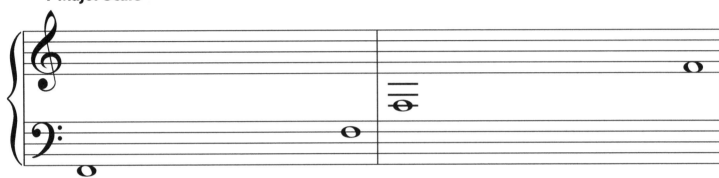

**B♭ Major Scale**

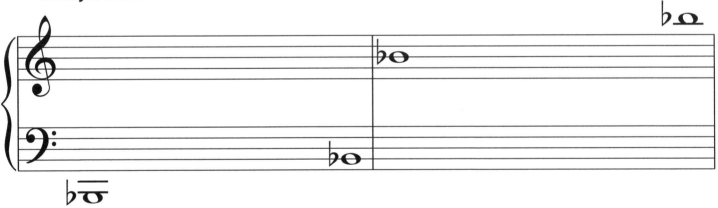

8. Fill in the blanks with the correct number.

    a. The C Major scale has _____ sharp(s) and _____ flat(s).

    b. The G Major scale has _____ sharp(s) and _____ flat(s).

    c. The D Major scale has _____ sharp(s) and _____ flat(s).

    d. The F Major scale has _____ sharp(s) and _____ flat(s).

    e. The B♭ Major scale has _____ sharp(s) and _____ flat(s). *Both B♭'s count as one flat.*

# Key Signatures

To make reading and writing music easier, the sharps or flats of the scale are written at the beginning of each staff. The **KEY SIGNATURE** tells you which notes are to be played sharp or flat throughout the piece.

The key signatures of the scales you already know are:

**C Major**
(No Sharps or Flats)

**G Major**
(One Sharp, F♯)

**D Major**
(Two Sharps, F♯ and C♯)

**F Major**
(One Flat, B♭)

**B♭ Major**
(Two Flats, B♭ and E♭)

1. Fill in the blanks with the correct answer.

    a. The key signature of _____ _____ has one flat, B♭.

    b. The key signature of _____ _____ has two flats, B♭ and E♭.

    c. The key signature of _____ _____ has one sharp, F♯.

    d. The key signature of _____ _____ has two sharps, F♯ and C♯.

    e. The key signature of _____ _____ has no sharps and no flats.

2. Name the Major key signatures.

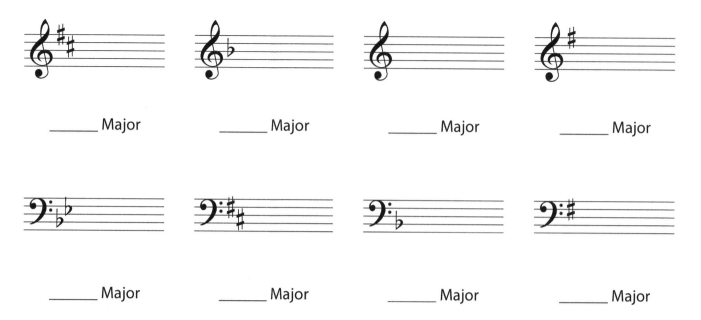

_____ Major        _____ Major        _____ Major        _____ Major

_____ Major        _____ Major        _____ Major        _____ Major

3. Draw the key signature named below each measure in both clefs. Then draw the tonic (key-note.) *The first one is done for you.*

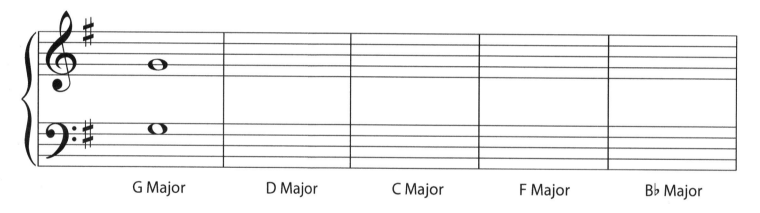

G Major          D Major          C Major          F Major          B♭ Major

4. In the following musical examples:

    a. Circle the notes to be played sharp or flat.
    b. Name the key signature.
    c. Play the music.

## Key of _____ Major

Key of _____ Major

Key of _____ Major

Key of _____ Major

Key of _____ Major

## Ear Training

1. You will hear four measures of rhythmic dictation. Fill in the blank measures with the rhythm you hear.

2. You will hear six intervals. Circle the interval you hear from each pair.

1. 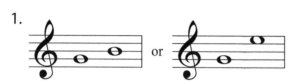    2.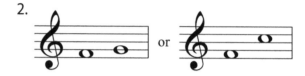

3. 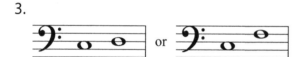    4.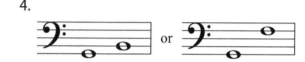

5. 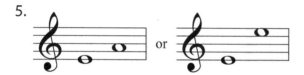    6.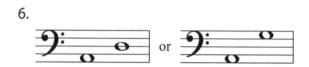

3. You will hear three notes in each group. The first two notes are given. Write the missing third note in each measure. *It will be a 2nd or 3rd lower or higher than the last note given.*

1. 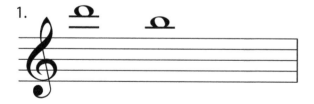    2.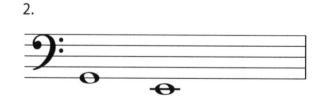

3. 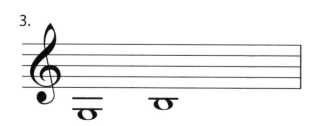    4.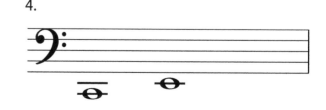

# 12-Bar Blues Improvisation

You may have heard a 12-bar blues harmonic pattern before. The **BLUES** originated in America over one hundred years ago, and it remains the most popular form in jazz music.

You can create your own 12-bar blues piece by following these steps:

1. Practice the bass clef intervals below. Each measure contains this pattern: 5th, 6th and 7th.

2. Review the G Major and G minor 5-finger patterns. They will form the basis for your right hand improvisation.

3. Begin by playing hands together, with the right hand stepping up and down in quarter notes.

4. Make up your own right hand improvisation over the left hand harmonic pattern to create your own 12-bar blues improvisation.

# Term Quiz

1. Mark each statement as either true or false.

_____ a. The interval of a 6th skips five keys on the keyboard.

_____ b. ♩. ♪ equals two beats.

_____ c. An upbeat comes after the first full measure of a piece.

_____ d. Intervals that move from line to line or space to space are always even numbers.

_____ e. The key signature tells which notes to play sharp or flat throughout a piece.

_____ f. In a Major scale, the half steps are between scale degrees 3-4 and 7-8.

_____ g. An interval of an octave skips six keys on the keyboard.

2. Fill in the blank with the correct number or letter.

a. The key signature of D Major has _____ sharps.

b. The third note of the F Major scale is _____.

c. The key signature of B♭ Major has _____ flats.

d. The C Major scale has _____ sharps and flats.

e. The _____ Major scale has one flat.

f. Every Major scale has _____ half steps.

g. The tonic of a G Major scale is _____.

h. The root of a C Major triad is _____.

i. The third of a D minor triad is _____.

j. The fifth of a B♭ minor triad is _____.

# Musical Signs and Terms

An asterisk (*) indicates words that are new to this book.

**DYNAMIC** signs tell how soft or loud to play the music.

| Italian Name | Sign (Symbol) | Meaning |
|---|---|---|
| pianissimo | *pp* | very soft |
| fortissimo | *ff* | very loud |
| crescendo (cresc.) | ![crescendo sign] | gradually louder |
| decrescendo or diminuendo (dim.) | ![decrescendo sign] | gradually softer |

**TEMPO** marks tell what speed to play the music.

| Italian Name | Meaning |
|---|---|
| ritardando (rit.) | gradually slower |
| a tempo | return to the original tempo |
| largo* | slow and broad, slower than *adagio* |
| andantino* | slightly faster than *andante* |
| allegretto* | moderately fast, slightly slower than *allegro* |
| vivace* | lively, quick |
| presto* | very fast |
| accelerando* (accel.) | becoming gradually faster |

1. In each blank write the dynamic sign to match the meaning.

   gradually louder _____    fortissimo _____

   pianissimo _____    gradually softer _____

2. In each blank write the Italian name for the following tempo marks.

very fast _____          slow and broad _____

becoming gradually faster _____

gradually slower _____          lively, quick _____

slightly faster than *andante* _____

return to the original tempo _____

moderately fast _____

**ARTICULATION** signs tell how to play and release the keys.

| Name | Sign (Symbol) | Meaning |
|---|---|---|
| accent | | play louder; emphasize |
| tenuto | | hold full value; stress |
| sforzando* | *sfz* or *sf* | sudden, strong accent |

The following terms help to describe the **mood** or **style** of the music.

| Italian Name | Meaning |
|---|---|
| dolce* | sweetly |
| grazioso* | gracefully |
| maestoso* | majestic; stately |
| poco* | little |
| molto* | very |

3. In each blank write the name that matches the meaning.

sudden, strong accent _____          little _____

sweetly _____          play louder; emphasize _____

very _____          majestic; stately _____

hold full value; stress _____          gracefully _____

# Other Musical Symbols

A **fermata** means to hold a note longer than its rhythmic value.

*8va*

An **octave sign** placed above the staff means to play one octave (eight notes) higher than written. An octave sign placed below the staff means to play one octave lower than written.

**Repeat signs** mean to play the music between the repeat signs again.

1.      2.

**1st and 2nd endings** mean to play the 1st ending and repeat from the beginning. Then skip over the 1st ending and play the 2nd ending.

The **pedal sign** shows when to press and release the damper pedal (right pedal).

**Dal segno\* (D.S.)** means to return to the sign 𝄋 .

**D.S. al Fine\*** means to return to the sign 𝄋 and play to *fine* (the end).

4. Clap the rhythm below. Return to the sign ( 𝄋 ) and stop at the end *(fine)*.

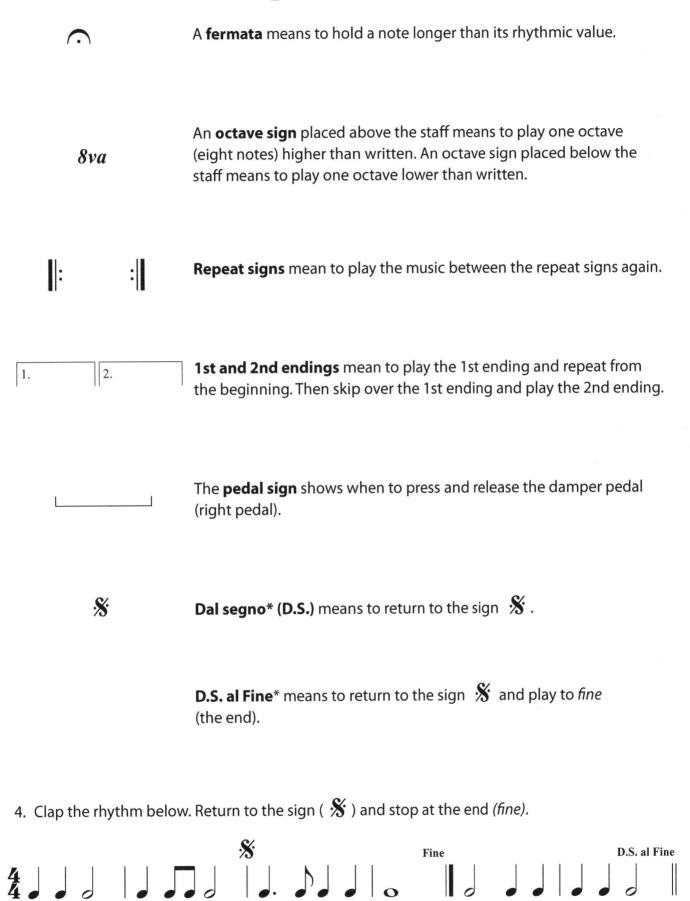

## REVIEW

1. Match each symbol or term with its definition by writing the correct letter in the blank.

| | | | |
|---|---|---|---|
| _____ | dolce | a. | very fast |
| _____ | presto | b. | slightly faster than *andante* |
| _____ | 𝄋 | c. | slow and broad |
| _____ | poco | d. | majestic; stately |
| _____ | andantino | e. | the sign |
| _____ | accelerando | f. | little |
| _____ | *sfz* or *sf* | g. | sweetly |
| _____ | maestoso | h. | return to 𝄋 and play to *fine* |
| _____ | largo | i. | very |
| _____ | vivace | j. | sudden, strong accent |
| _____ | molto | k. | gracefully |
| _____ | accent | l. | hold full value; stress |
| _____ | D.S. al Fine | m. | return to the beginning and play to *fine* |
| _____ | grazioso | n. | moderately fast |
| _____ | D.C. al Fine | o. | lively, quick |
| _____ | allegretto | p. | becoming gradually faster |
| _____ | tenuto | q. | play louder; emphasize |

2. Add all of the notes and rests as you would count them in $\frac{4}{4}$ time. Write the total number of beats in each box.

3. In each box draw one note to complete the measure.

4. Each rhythm below contains upbeats. Add bar lines to complete each example. Write the counts under the measures, then clap and count each pattern.

5. Write the letter name of each note in the blank below it. Write the number of the interval between the notes in each box.

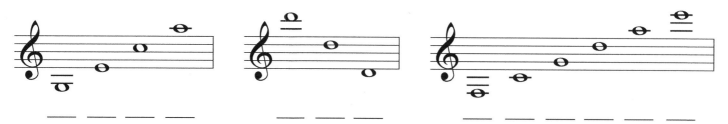

_____   _____   _____        _____   _____   _____        _____   _____   _____

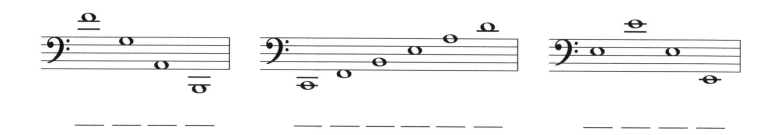

_____   _____   _____        _____   _____   _____   _____        _____   _____   _____

6. Draw a harmonic 6th down from the given note.

7. Draw a harmonic 7th up from the given note.

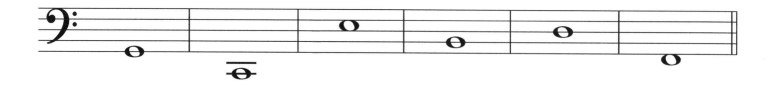

8. Draw a harmonic 8th (octave) down from the given note.

9. Draw a line connecting each key in Column A to its matching scale and key signature in Column B.

## Column A                                    ## Column B

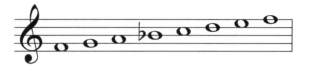

**C Major**

**D Major**

**F Major**

**G Major**

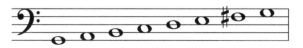

**B♭ Major**

# MUSICAL MASTERY

## Ear Training

1. You will hear one rhythm from each pair. Circle the rhythm you hear.

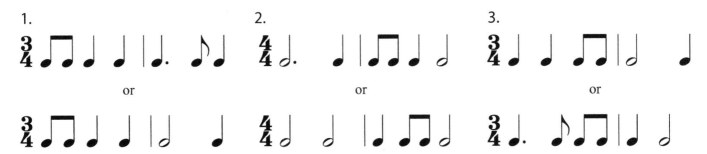

2. The first example in each pair is Major. The second example in each pair is minor. Circle the one you hear.

3. You will hear four measures of melodic dictation. Fill in the blank measures with the rhythms and pitches you hear.

4. You will hear intervals played in broken and blocked form. They will be either a 2nd, 5th or 7th. Write 2nd, 5th or 7th in the blank.

1._____  2._____  3._____  4._____  5._____  6._____

# Analysis

Study this excerpt from "Menuet in G Major," then answer the questions about it.

## Menuet in G Major

Christian Petzold
(1677-1733)

1. How many beats are in each measure? _____

2. Name the circled 5-finger pattern in measures 1 and 2. _____

3. How many measures contain a dotted half note? _____

4. Name the circled melodic interval in measure 4. _____

5. Name the triad in measure 1. _____

6. What is the tempo? _____

7. How many measures contain the rhythm ♩ ♫ ♫ ? _____

8. Do the circled eighth notes in measure 3 form a whole step or a half step? _____

9. How many F♯'s are there? _____

10. Name the circled melodic interval in measure 8. _____

# Symbol Mastery

Unscramble the words to complete each sentence.

1. A note that comes before the first full measure of a piece is called an _____.
   *paubte*

2. Melodic _____ are two notes played separately to make a melody.
   *tservnial*

3. A dotted quarter note is usually followed by an _____ _____.
   *ihgthe*          *teno*

4. The D Major scale has two _____.
   *hpasrs*

5. _____ _____ extend the range of the staff.
   *dgelre*          *nsile*

6. The keynote or _____ is the first note of a scale.
   *oticn*

7. Eight notes above or below a note makes an _____.
   *ovetca*

8. The bottom note of a triad is called the _____.
   *toro*

9. The F Major scale has one _____.
   *ltaf*

10. A _____ _____ has half steps between scale degrees 3-4 and 7-8.
    *jmoar*          *lasce*

11. The _____ _____ tells which notes to play sharp or flat throughout
    *yke*          *nursgteia*
    a piece.

12. An interval of a seventh skips _____ keys on the keyboard.
    *ivef*

13. _____ marks tell what speed to play the music.
    *mopet*

14. The time signature tells how many beats are in each _____.
    *esurmae*

# THEORY MASTERY

## Review Test

1. On the staff below, draw the notes or rests that are named below each measure.

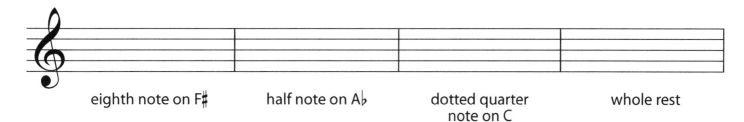

eighth note on F♯    half note on A♭    dotted quarter
note on C    whole rest

2. Write the name of each interval in the blank below it.

3. Draw the note that completes the harmonic interval above the given note.

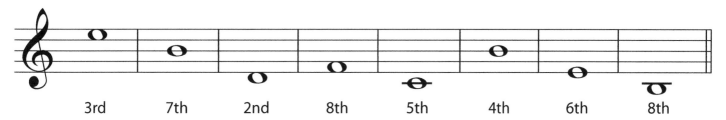

3rd    7th    2nd    8th    5th    4th    6th    8th

4. Transpose this melody to the G Major 5-finger pattern. *Keep the rhythms and intervals the same.*
   *Remember the stem rule.*

5. Draw bar lines where they are needed.

6. Write the counts below each measure.

7. Write the top number of the time signature in each measure below. Choose from these time signatures. $\frac{2}{4}$ $\frac{3}{4}$ $\frac{4}{4}$ $\frac{5}{4}$ $\frac{6}{4}$

8. Add the correct sharps or flats to form these Major scales. Mark the half steps with a curved line. Circle the tonic (keynote.)

**D Major Scale**

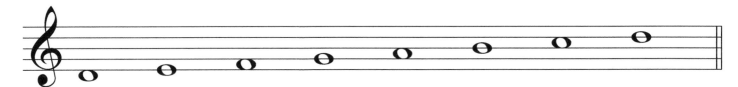

**B♭ Major Scale**

**G Major Scale**

**F Major Scale**

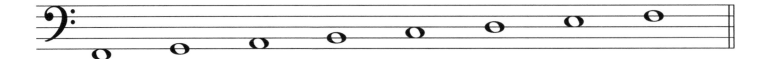

9. Name the Major key signatures.

_____Major      _____Major      _____Major      _____Major      _____Major

10. Write the letter of the correct definition in the blank beside each term.

| | | |
|---|---|---|
| _____ D.C. al Fine | a. | the distance between two notes |
| _____ accelerando | b. | sudden, strong accent |
| _____ interval | c. | return to the beginning and stop at *fine* |
| _____ minor 5-finger pattern | d. | short lines above or below the staff |
| _____ ledger lines | e. | W  W  H  W  W  W  H |
| _____ sforzando | f. | becoming gradually faster |
| _____ D.S. al Fine | g. | an interval of eight notes |
| _____ Major scale | h. | W  W  H  W |
| _____ tonic | i. | change a piece from one key to another |
| _____ octave | j. | W  H  W  W |
| _____ triad | k. | return to the sign and stop at *fine* |
| _____ transpose | l. | first note of a scale |
| _____ Major 5-finger pattern | m. | chord made up of a root, third and fifth |

# Ear Training

1. You will hear four measures of rhythmic dictation. Fill in the blank measures with the rhythm you hear.

2. You will hear a Major or minor triad played in broken and blocked form. Circle the one you hear.

**1. Major or minor**      **2. Major or minor**      **3. Major or minor**

**4. Major or minor**      **5. Major or minor**      **6. Major or minor**

3. You will hear one interval from each pair. Circle the interval you hear.

a.

or

b.
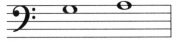

c.

or

d.
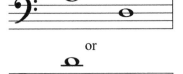
or

4. You will hear four measures of melodic dictation. Fill in the blank measures with the notes and rhythms you hear.